better together*

* This book is best read together, grownup and kid.

akidsco.com

a kids book about

a kids book about PURPOSE

by Karina LeBlanc

A Kids Book About
Editor Emma Wolf
Head of Design Rick DeLucco
Publisher Jelani Memory

DK
Senior Production Editor Jennifer Murray
Senior Production Controller Louise Minihane
Managing Editor Hazel Eriksson
Publishing Director Mark Searle

This American Edition, 2026
Published in the United States by DK Publishing,
a Division of Penguin Random House LLC
1745 Broadway, 20th Floor, New York, NY 10019

26 27 28 29 10 9 8 7 6 5 4 3 2 1
001—355682—Feb/26

First published in Great Britain in 2026 by
Dorling Kindersley Limited, 20 Vauxhall Bridge Road, London SW1V 2SA
A Penguin Random House Company

The authorised representative in the EEA is
Dorling Kindersley Verlag GmbH. Arnulfstr. 124, 80636 Munich, Germany

A CIP catalogue record for this book is available from the British Library

ISBN 978-0-2417-8592-8

Printed and bound in China

www.dk.com

akidsco.com

This book was made with Forest Stewardship Council™ certified paper – one small step in DK's commitment to a sustainable future.
Learn more at www.dk.com/uk/information/sustainability

For my daughter, Paris.

You are my heart, my why,
and my forever purpose.

May you always chase your dreams
and live boldly into the greatness
that's already inside of you.

Intro
for grownups

Hi grownups, thanks for picking up this book. We're about to dive into something big—purpose. Not in a pressure-filled, figure-it-all-out kind of way, but in the way that gets kids thinking, "What lights me up?"

As a former Olympic athlete, I used to think my purpose was about winning. But as I grew, I learned it was more about impact—how I showed up for others—especially when it was hard. This story is about the journey of finding that kind of purpose through sports, failure, courage, and giving 15 extra minutes a day.

Whether you're reading this to your kid, a classroom, or a team, I hope it sparks big dreams and honest conversations. Because every kid has a purpose, and they deserve to believe in it.

With heart,
Karina

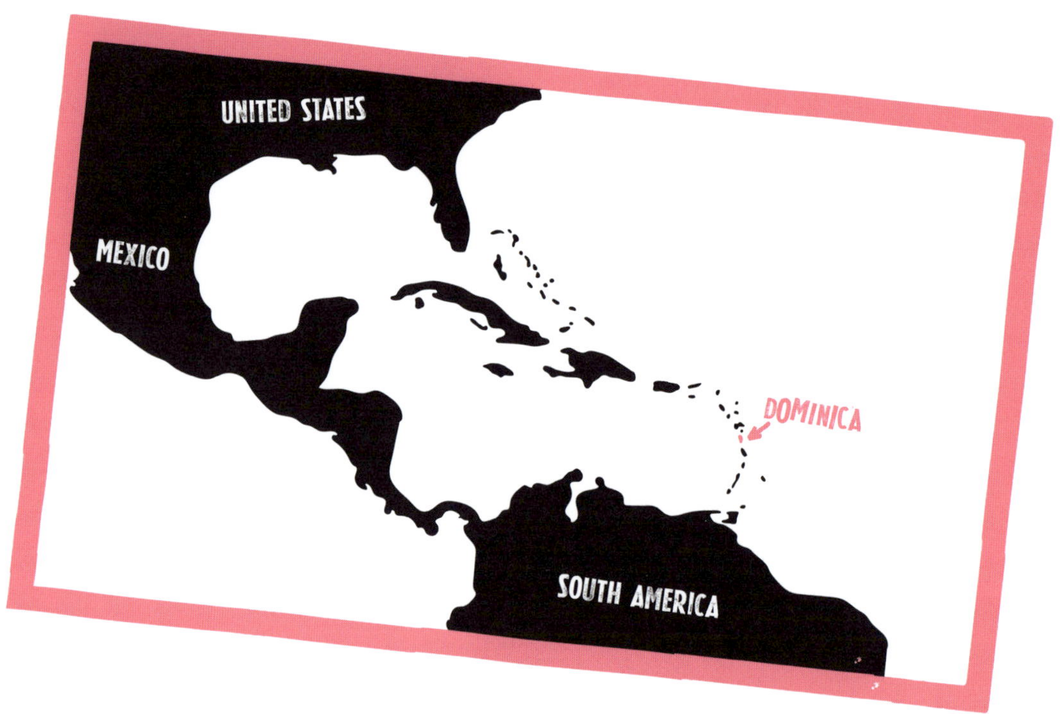

I grew up on a small island called Dominica, but I was actually born in the USA.

Right before I was born, there was a

HUGE **hurricane.**

So we fled to our aunt's house in Georgia until our roof got put back on.

Basically, what I'm saying is I came into the world in a

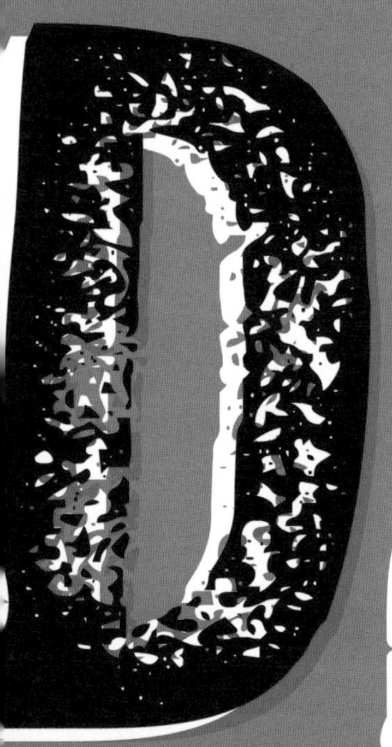

and honestly, that's still kind of how I live today.

This is my book all about

PURPOSE.

(I'm Karina, by the way!)

Have you ever felt like you were meant to do something really

Me too!

For me...

PURPOSE helps you understand why your life matters.

PURPOSE is the thing you can go back to when life gets tough.

PURPOSE is how you leave an impact on the world.

And more than anything,

PURPOSE is how you understand the greatness inside of you.

(Yes, you, the kid reading this book right now!)

So, let's dive in! 

When I was 8 years old, my family moved from Dominica to Canada.

We went from a place where everyone looked like me...

to a place where everyone was different from me.

Almost everyone was white, and no one understood me with my thick accent.

It was hard.

I was called dirty
because my skin was Black.

That hurt.

I remember complaining
to my parents,

"Why did you do this to us?"

Looking back, I now see a really important life skill my parents were teaching me:

RTABLE

ORTABLE.

This was the first time I realized that I would have to do **hard things to achieve what I wanted**.

And what I really wanted...

WAS TO BE AN

OLYMPIAN!

I loved everything about playing sports, especially the **connections I made with my teammates**.

Moving and starting over
was hard and uncomfortable.

But soccer helped me be **brave**
and **get out of my comfort zone**.

I still remember the first team I played for.

We had these gray jerseys
I was so proud to wear and
represent our little team.

As I grew up,
I got pretty good at soccer.

I was having fun, playing well,
winning games, and eventually,
I got to try out for the U15 team,
which was a **BIG** deal.

This was my next step toward
my dream of being an Olympian.

And guess what?

I tried out...

OT CUT

I was

DEVAS

I was so

EMBAR

I remember driving home and crying to my parents.

TATED.

RASSED.

My dad turned to me and said, **"Well, what are you going to do about it?"**

I took that challenge to heart.

And the way I did that was simple:

do 15 minutes more,

PRACTICE HARD...
and then do 15 minutes more.

FINISH MY HOMEWORK...
and then head outside for
15 minutes more of soccer.

I gave 15 minutes more every day
so I could go from **GOOD** to **GREAT**.

I put in the work and I started
to truly believe in myself.

The next year, I tried out for an
even better team, and I made it.

Giving 15 minutes more taught
me that every dream I wanted
to achieve was going to be about
doing something hard instead
of choosing something easy.

I eventually did get to the Olympics.

TWICE, IN FACT!

Getting comfortable
being uncomfortable,
and doing 15 minutes more,
helped me achieve
an amazing goal.

And chasing my dreams
helped me discover that purpose
isn't just about what you achieve...

it's about

WHO YOU
ALONG

BECOME THE WAY.

After my team won a medal at the London Olympics, my coach pulled me aside to have a conversation that changed my life.

He said, **"If you think your purpose is to kick a soccer ball, then I've failed you."**

I WAS STRUCK.

I thought that **WAS** my purpose.

But I realized that winning the medal wasn't the end of something—**it was the start.**

While I had achieved my dream,
I now had a purpose to live into.

FAST FORWARD a few years and a thousand miles from home, I was in Honduras to teach soccer to a group of girls.

We were in a place with much more crime than I had grown up knowing, and we practiced soccer on gravel, not grass.

But still, they came to play soccer with me.

They didn't really know who I was, but because I showed up for them, they were eager to learn.

And my time with those girls was incredible.

A WILD THING HAPPENED THERE THAT DAY.

Remember those gray jerseys from that little team I first played for?

Some of the girls were wearing those exact same jerseys* I wore on my first team.

*Turns out, they had been donated to the kids by a Canadian charity years earlier!

That's when I knew
I wasn't just living my dream,
I was living my purpose.

I realized I was exactly where
I was meant to be, doing exactly
what I was meant to be doing.

**Have you ever had
a moment like that?**

You may not know your purpose yet,

AND THAT'S OK.

Your dreams matter, and going after them can help you discover the greatness that lives inside of you.

Start by asking yourself:

WHAT MAKES ME FEEL EXCITED?

WHAT DO I LOVE DOING?

WHAT MAKES ME FEEL ALIVE?

WHAT DO I WANT TO HELP MAKE BETTER IN THE WORLD?

Your answer to these questions can guide your dreams and help lead you to your purpose.

Because here's what I've learned:

**When you show up,
especially when it's hard,
you start discovering
who you really are.**

THAT'S WHERE YOUR PURPOSE LIVES.

So,

dream crazy big,

work hard,

believe in yourself,

forgive yourself when you make a mistake,

be kind,

and never forget that there is a unique greatness inside of you.

The world needs you,

JUST AS

YOU ARE.

Purpose doesn't
show up all at once.

But every step you take brings
you a bit closer to the person

ANT TO BE.

Outro
for grownups

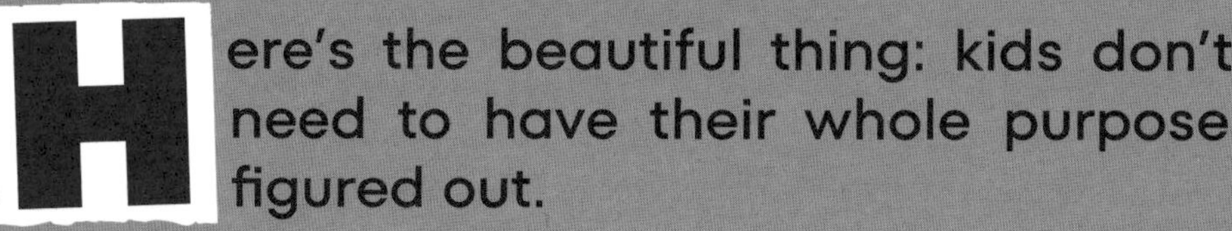

Here's the beautiful thing: kids don't need to have their whole purpose figured out.

They just need space to ask questions, explore what excites them, and try new things. Purpose doesn't always arrive with a big moment. Sometimes, it's found in quiet consistency, showing up, being kind, and doing a little more each day.

My journey started with sport, but yours might look different. The goal isn't perfection, it's growth. So as the grownup in their life, you have the power to model that for them—to cheer them on, challenge them, and remind them they're already enough.

Maybe you're still discovering your purpose too! That's OK. You're not late. You're living it, one step at a time.

Keep going. They're watching, and learning, from you.

About The Author

Karina LeBlanc (she/her) is a two-time Olympian, a bronze medalist, and a trailblazer in the world of women's sports. Born in the US, raised in the Caribbean and Canada, she found her purpose through sport and has spent her life helping others find theirs. From the soccer field to the global stage, Karina's mission is to empower the next generation of leaders. She wrote this book to inspire kids, especially those who feel different, unseen, or unsure of their path, to believe in their greatness and take small steps toward a bigger purpose.

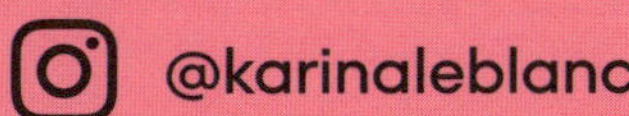

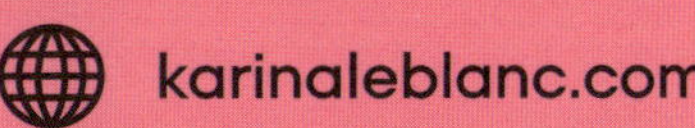